CAMP

Journal

An Activity Book and Record Keeper

BY SUSAN HOOD

PETER PAUPER PRESS, INC.
WHITE PLAINS, NEW YORK

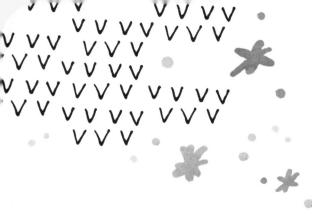

PETER PAUPER PRESS

In 1928, at the age of twenty-two, Peter Beilenson began printing books on a small press in the basement of his parents' home in Larchmont, New York. Peter—and later, his wife, Edna—sought to create fine books that sold at "prices even a pauper could afford."

Today, still family owned and operated, Peter Pauper Press continues to honor our founders' legacy of quality, value, and fun for big kids and small kids alike.

Designed by Heather Zschock

Copyright © 2018
Peter Pauper Press, Inc.
Manufactured for Peter Pauper Press, Inc.
202 Mamaroneck Avenue
White Plains, NY 10601 USA
All rights reserved
ISBN 978-1-4413-2637-9
Printed in China

Published in the United Kingdom and Europe by
Peter Pauper Press, Inc. c/o White Pebble International
Unit 2, Plot 11 Terminus Road
Chichester, West Sussex PO19 8TX, UK

7 6 5 4 3 2 1

Visit us at www.peterpauper.com

CONTENTS

Away We Go!

I'm off to camp:
_____

Located in:
_____

Here's how I'm getting there:
_____

_____

_____

Here's what I hope to do at camp:
_____

_____

_____

_____

_____

_____

_____

_____

_____

_____

Here's Me!

(Paste photo or draw picture here.)

Games to Go!

Whether you're travelling by car, bus, or airplane, or just hanging out with your friends, these games will keep you entertained!

ALPHABETICAL PROPER NAMES

OBJECTIVE: Start with a girl's or boy's first name that begins with the letter A. Play continues in alphabetical order until someone can't think of a name within the 30-second time limit.

VARIATIONS: Names starting with the letters Q, X, and Z can be skipped.

FAMOUS NAMES

OBJECTIVE: Players take turns thinking of famous people, and stating the first letter of the famous person's name (or the person's initials). By asking "yes or no" questions, the other players try to guess the identity of the famous person. The player who guesses correctly chooses the next famous person.

GHOST

OBJECTIVE: The first player chooses a starter letter. The person to the left then adds a letter, being careful not to make a word. This continues until someone is forced to make a word or passes the 30-second time limit. The person who loses the round has a "G." The other players have a clean slate. The first player to lose 5 rounds is knocked out (G-H-O-S-T).

NOTE: Each player must have a longer word in mind when he or she adds a letter, and can be "challenged" by the next player.

EXAMPLE:

Player 1-a / Player 2-p (ap)
Player 3-p (app) / Player 4-l (appl)
Player 5-e (apple) loses

If player 5 had added an i (appli) the game would have continued.

LETTER WORDS

OBJECTIVE: Players try to think of four-letter words. Play continues until someone can't think of a word within the 30-second time limit.

VARIATIONS: Three-letter words can be used for younger children.

Name the Sports Teams

OBJECTIVE: Players take turns naming different sports teams until someone can't think of one within the 30-second time limit.

VARIATIONS: Proceed in alphabetical order, skipping Q, X, Z.

Number List

MATERIALS: Pencil, paper

OBJECTIVE: Players take turns saying a number smaller than 10. Have someone write them down in order as you go along. Each player must list all of the numbers previously said, and then add another number. Play continues until someone forgets or mixes up the order.

Odd and Even

OBJECTIVE: All players pick whether they are "odd numbers" or "even numbers." At the count of three each puts out anywhere from 1 to 5 fingers. After the fingers are added, if the total number is odd, the odd players win. If it is even, the even players win. Award points to the winners of each round. The first player(s) to get 20 points wins.

Round Robin Storytelling

OBJECTIVE: One player begins with the first sentence of a story. Each player then adds a sentence, until all the players together have invented a story. The story should continue through one or more rounds of players, until it reaches "The End." The story can be as realistic or as silly as the players wish.

Scavenger Hunt

MATERIALS: Pencil, paper

OBJECTIVE: Before the game begins, decide upon a list of objects to search for. Each person who spots one of the objects receives a point. Play until someone gets 20 points or the trip ends.

EXAMPLE: Possible objects to hunt for could be an out-of-state plate, farm stand, canoe, duck, or dragonfly.

Yes or No

OBJECTIVE: One person thinks of an item. He or she lets the other players know what type of item it is—for example, an animal, place, or thing. Other players have 25 chances combined to ask questions or guess the item. The person who is "it" can only answer "Yes" or "No," so questions must be worded appropriately. The player who guesses correctly is then "it" and chooses the next item.

My Head Counselor

Name: Da

Age: 18

Hometown or country: Virginua

Best thing about my counselor: she is ~~new~~
~~She~~ kind sweet.

My counselor always says: That she's
52 and she also
~~say~~ says she's very tierd

Rate your counselor.

- ● Sweet
- ○ Crazy
- ● Funny
- ○ A Big Boss
- ○ Scary
- ● Way Cool
- ○ Lame
- ○ Whacked
- ○ Geek
- ○ Nerd
- ● Diva
- ○ Dude

My Head Counselor

(Paste photo or draw picture here.)

MY OTHER COUNSELORS

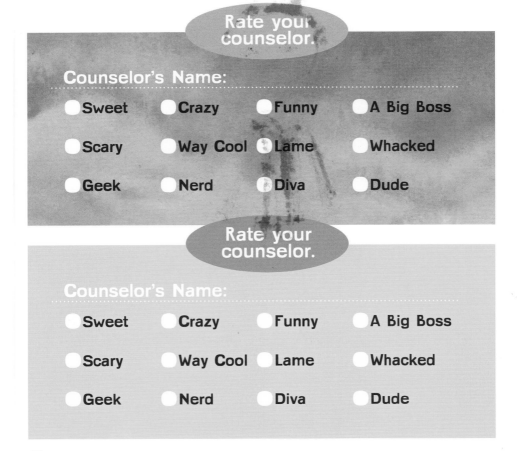

Rate your counselor.

Counselor's Name:

◯ Sweet ◯ Crazy ◯ Funny ◯ A Big Boss

◯ Scary ◯ Way Cool ◯ Lame ◯ Whacked

◯ Geek ◯ Nerd ◯ Diva ◯ Dude

Rate your counselor.

Counselor's Name:

◯ Sweet ◯ Crazy ◯ Funny ◯ A Big Boss

◯ Scary ◯ Way Cool ◯ Lame ◯ Whacked

◯ Geek ◯ Nerd ◯ Diva ◯ Dude

Rate your counselor.

Counselor's Name:

- ⚪ Sweet
- ⚪ Crazy
- ⚪ Funny
- ⚪ A Big Boss
- ⚪ Scary
- ⚪ Way Cool
- ⚪ Lame
- ⚪ Whacked
- ⚪ Geek
- ⚪ Nerd
- ⚪ Diva
- ⚪ Dude

Rate your counselor.

Counselor's Name:

- ⚪ Sweet
- ⚪ Crazy
- ⚪ Funny
- ⚪ A Big Boss
- ⚪ Scary
- ⚪ Way Cool
- ⚪ Lame
- ⚪ Whacked
- ⚪ Geek
- ⚪ Nerd
- ⚪ Diva
- ⚪ Dude

Rate your counselor.

Counselor's Name:

- ⚪ Sweet
- ⚪ Crazy
- ⚪ Funny
- ⚪ A Big Boss
- ⚪ Scary
- ⚪ Way Cool
- ⚪ Lame
- ⚪ Whacked
- ⚪ Geek
- ⚪ Nerd
- ⚪ Diva
- ⚪ Dude

My Bunk

Here's where I'll hang out for the next _____ **weeks.**

(Paste photo or draw picture of camp cabin/tent/bunkhouse here.)

It's: ⬤ great   ⬤ gross   ⬤ gruesome
       ⬤ grand   ⬤ groovy   ⬤ goofy

Here's a list of my bunkmates:

_____

_____

_____

_____

_____

(Paste photo or draw
picture of bunk and
bunkmates here.)

My Schedule

	MONDAY	TUESDAY	WEDNESDAY
TIME			
Activity			
Location			
Love it/Hate it			
TIME			
Activity			
Location			
Love it/Hate it			
TIME			
Activity			
Location			
Love it/Hate it			
TIME			
Activity			
Location			
Love it/Hate it			
TIME			
Activity			
Location			
Love it/Hate it			
TIME			
Activity			
Location			
Love it/Hate it			
TIME			
Activity			
Location			
Love it/Hate it			

THURSDAY	FRIDAY	SATURDAY	SUNDAY

My Picks

My ultimate favorite activity is

Runners up are

The best rainy day activity is

The coolest camp song or cheer is

My ultimate least favorite activity is

The best trip/outing of the summer so far

Icebreaker

To break the ice on the first day of camp, have your new buds fill in
the blanks without looking. Then read the story out loud.

THE FIRST Day OF CaMP...

We arrived at Camp _____ at _____ o'clock. The first
　　　　　　　　　　　　 (noun)　　　　　　 (number)

thing I saw was the _____
　　　　　　　　　　 (adjective)

and I got very _____ .
(noun)　　　　　　　　　　　　　　 (adjective)

I walked to Cabin _____ . There I met three kids,
　　　　　　　　　　 (noun)

named _____ , _____ ,
　　　 (animal)　　　　　 (friend's name)

and _____ . They were very _____
　　 (type of car)　　　　　　　　　　　 (adjective)

and helped me unpack my _____ . Then we
　　　　　　　　　　　　 (noun)

_____ to lunch at the _____ hall.
(past-tense verb)　　　　　　　　　 (noun)

We were crowding around the _____ , when out came
　　　　　　　　　　　　　 (noun)

a(n) _____ . It chased us out the door,
　 (noun)

around the _____ and all the way to _____ .
　　　　　 (plural noun)　　　　　　　　　 (favorite vacation spot)

We finally got it to go away by feeding it _____
　　　　　　　　　　　　　　　　　 (least favorite food)

and pushing it into Lake _____ . It's been a(n)
　　　　　　　　　　 (proper noun)

_____ start to camp and I'm _____
(adjective)　　　　　　　　　　　　　 (adjective)

about the rest of the summer!

Read My Palm

You can tell a lot about people by looking at their palms. So when you're doing all those "nice-to-meet-you" handshakes, take a closer look. How long is the life line? How about the heart (love) line? Use the palms on these pages to map your friends' futures (and yours, too)!

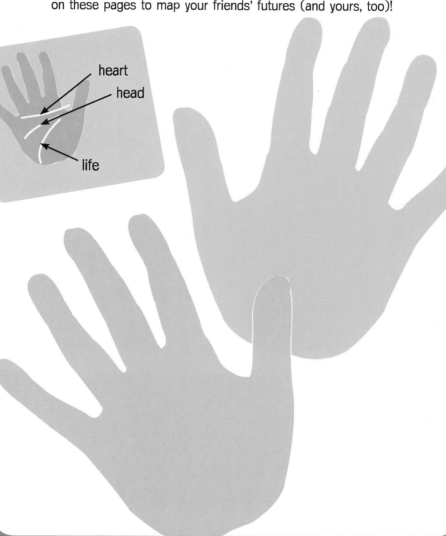

heart
head
life

If the heart line has lots of branches—
you're a real charmer! Of course lots of breaks
in the line can symbolize lots of breakups.
But if you've got a long, straight, deep heart line,
it can mean that when you fall in love with
someone, you'll love them for a long time.

Why did
Jennifer pour
ketchup on
her hand?

She needed her
palm read.

If your life line has branches facing upward, you'll have good health and success. Look for breaks in the life line—it can mean sudden changes (good or bad).

If the head line is strong and deep that can mean the person is very straightforward and logical. On the other hand (no pun intended!) if the head line is faint, you might be dealing with a person who has a wandering mind and difficulty paying attention.

Let's Talk!

What do you think? What do your friends think?

	COOL	NOT COOL
Musical Artists		
Songs		

	COOL	NOT COOL
Movies		
Celebs		

	COOL	NOT COOL
TV Shows		
Books		

	COOL	NOT COOL
Video Games		
Other		

And the Next Big Thing is...

BELLY LAUGHS

Best Jokes I Heard at Camp:

Why wouldn't the skeleton dive into the pool?

He didn't have the guts.

Why do seagulls fly over the sea?

Because if they flew over the bay, they'd be bagels.

What do you get if you cross a parrot with a centipede?

A walkie talkie.

29

Pack it up

**Before you head out on a hike,
don't forget your hiker's emergency kit:**

- whistle
- trail map
- shatterproof mirror
- mylar blanket
- water bottle
- sunscreen
- bug repellent
- small flashlight
- compass
- snack
- a buddy

WHAT ELSE?

- _____
- _____
- _____
- _____
- _____
- _____
- _____
- _____
- _____
- _____

**P.S. If you go out hiking on your own,
don't forget to tell someone where you're
going and when you'll be back.**

If you get lost:

- Stay calm and stay put.
- Blow your whistle in three short bursts every few minutes.
- Flash your mirror: three short flashes, three long flashes, three short flashes—that's Morse code for S.O.S.

WALK THIS WAY!

To mark your trail so others can follow
(or so that you can find your way back),
just use any of the following signs:

These signs mean "turn right."

- grass tips tied together and bent to right
- stick in fork of tree pointing to right
- two stones on left and one stone on right

These mean "turn left."

- grass tips tied together and bent to left
- stick in fork of tree pointing to left
- two stones on right and one stone on left

This means "do not go this way."

- sticks crossed

P.P.S. Make sure you've equipped yourself with
good, comfortable hiking shoes—ones that grip,
not glide. (Flip-flops need not apply!)

CAMPER BEWARE!

Learn to ID and avoid these pesky plants or you'll be sorry! Brushing against these poisonous plants can cause an itchy, awful rash.

REMEMBER: "LEAVES OF THREE, LET IT BE!"

Poison Ivy   Poison Oak   Poison Sumac

RX: If you do touch one of these plants by mistake, wash the plant's oils off with soap as soon as possible. Ask your counselor to treat the area with alcohol. If a rash develops, go to the infirmary.

FIRST AID Tips I've Learned:

RIGHT ON TRACK

What animals have you spotted this summer?

- squirrel
- deer
- raccoon
- rabbit
- mouse
- seagull
- fox
- chipmunk
- cat
- dog
- hedgehog
- blue jay
- chickadee
- horse

Can you find the following?

- ladybug
- cricket
- mosquito
- firefly
- spider
- centipede
- wasp
- dragonfly
- caterpillar
- ant
- bee
- moth

TICKS TICK ME OFF!

Ticks can cause Rocky Mountain spotted fever and
Lyme disease, so if you see one, tell your counselor!
Look carefully all over your body after a hike.
Ticks like to hide in dark places like in your hair
and under your armpits. They're tiny! In fact,
deer ticks can be as small as the period at the
end of this sentence.

Look What I Found . . .

(Press or sketch your favorite plants here.)

Can you find:
- **Queen Anne's Lace**
- **Buttercup**
- **Dandelion**
- **Violet**
- **Daisy**
- **Forget-Me-Not**
- **Clover**
- **Honeysuckle**
- **Sunflower**
- **Wild Rose**

How to Make a Daisy Chain

Slit a 1-inch-long part of the stem of a daisy with your fingernail, close to the flower. Pull another stem through the hole. Make a slit in the second stem and pull a third stem though it. Continue until you have enough for a bracelet, a necklace, or a crown.

WHAT'S FOR LUNCH?

Camp Food Faves:

Camp Food Flops:

WHAT'S FOR DINNER?

Camp Food Faves:

Camp Food Flops:

Starry Starry Night

When the stars come out, look for these constellations in the night sky. Look for the Big Dipper first. Once you find it, follow the arrows to find the others.

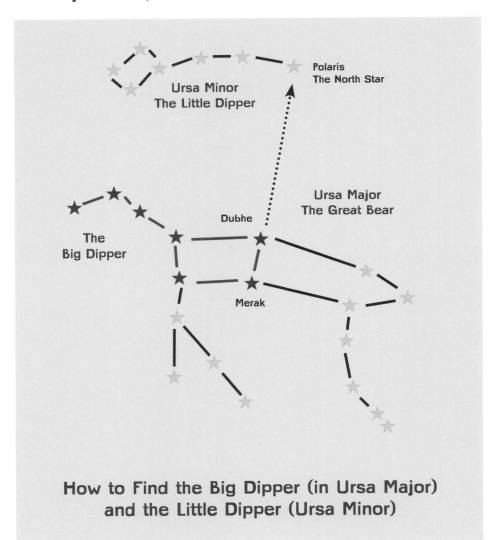

Polaris
The North Star

Ursa Minor
The Little Dipper

Ursa Major
The Great Bear

Dubhe

The
Big Dipper

Merak

How to Find the Big Dipper (in Ursa Major) and the Little Dipper (Ursa Minor)

How to Find:

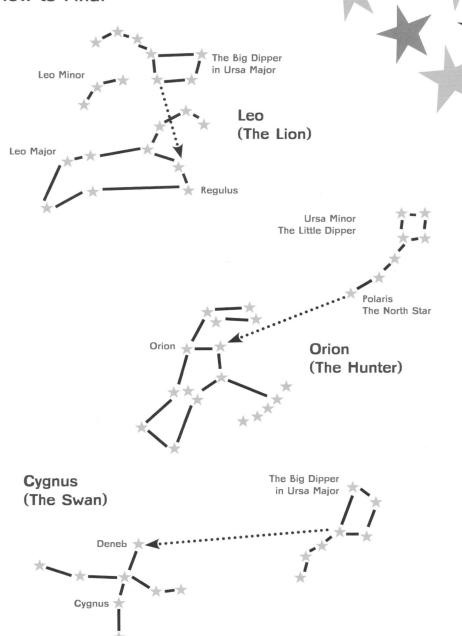

Leo Minor

The Big Dipper
in Ursa Major

**Leo
(The Lion)**

Leo Major

Regulus

Ursa Minor
The Little Dipper

Polaris
The North Star

Orion

**Orion
(The Hunter)**

**Cygnus
(The Swan)**

The Big Dipper
in Ursa Major

Deneb

Cygnus

AROUND THE CAMPFIRE

S'MORES... as in, "Gimme some more!"
Everything tastes better when made on the campfire.
1. Place a plain chocolate bar on top of a graham cracker.
2. Next, put a hot roasted marshmallow on top of the chocolate bar.
3. Top the marshmallow with another graham cracker and dig in!

MURDER WINK
Count out as many playing cards as there are players. Be sure to include the Jack of Spades. Whoever gets the Jack is the murderer and should keep that fact a secret. Return all the cards to the center.

TO PLAY: The murderer tries to catch each person's eye, then winks and that person must fall over dead. If you can guess who the murderer is, shout out the name before they wink at you. If you're right, you win. If you're wrong, you're out!

SINGING AROUND THE CAMPFIRE
Write the words to your favorite tunes here:

How many of these
Campfire Classics can
you sing?

Michael Row the Boat Ashore
If I Had a Hammer
This Land Is Your Land
Blowin' in the Wind
Kumbaya
Five Hundred Miles

TRUTH OR DARE?

Assemble the Cootie Catcher on the next page, and it will determine your fate!

To play:

Ask one friend in the group to pick a word on the Cootie Catcher. Spell out the word, moving your fingers in and out for each letter. Then ask your friend to pick a number. Count to that number, moving your fingers in and out. Your friend then chooses a final number. Lift the flap under the number to determine which "truth" or "dare" they get. If your friend answers the question or does the dare, pass them the Cootie Catcher. If not, they are out for the rest of the game. (You can make up new "truths" or "dares", too.)

Truth #1: What would you do with $1,000?
Truth #2: What's your biggest secret?
Truth #3: What was the most embarrassing thing that ever happened to you?
Truth #4: What's the worst thing you've ever done?

Truth #1:

Truth #2:

Truth #3:

Truth #4:

Dare #1: Shortsheet someone's bed. *(See page 45.)*
Dare #2: Attempt a cartwheel.
Dare #3: Wear your shirt inside out all day tomorrow.
Dare #4: Let a bug crawl up your arm.

Dare #1:

Dare #2:

Dare #3:

Dare #4:

Cootie Catcher

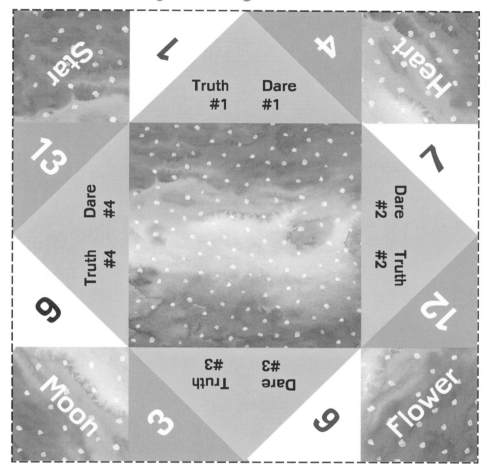

To assemble the cootie catcher:

1. Pull the Cootie Catcher out of your book.
2. Cut along the dotted line to create a square piece of paper. Turn it face down.
3. Fold the four corners to the middle.
4. Turn the square over. Fold these four corners to the middle.
5. Then fold in half.
6. Open and fold in half the other way.
7. Insert fingers under the flaps.

Lights Out

When it's lights out time, there's still time for fun and games!

Shortsheeting a Bed

1. Remove the blanket and top sheet. Put the top sheet back on the bed and tuck it in at the top of the bed only, over the bottom sheet.
2. Fold the bottom of the top sheet 2/3 of the way back up.
3. Replace the blanket neatly, fold the bottom of the top sheet over it, and tuck everything in so it looks normal.

Shadow Plays

Hang up a sheet. Shine a flashlight onto the sheet from behind it. Enact scenes from your favorite movies and books between the light and the sheet. (The audience sits in front of the sheet.)

Story in the Dark

One person starts with a sentence, such as, "One night a girl heard a scream in the woods." The person in the next bed adds a sentence and so on around the cabin.

Categories

One person chooses a category—Scary Movies, for example. Go around the cabin naming as many scary movies as you can. If you can't think of any, you're out! The person in the next bed names the next category.

Or, invent some of your own:

Dream Catcher

The dream I remember most:

_____

_____

_____

_____

_____

_____

_____

_____

_____

_____

_____

_____

_____

_____

_____

_____

_____

_____

_____

_____

_____

_____

_____

_____

_____

Other dreams:

_____

_____

_____

_____

_____

_____

_____

_____

_____

_____

CAMP DEEDS

Something I did that was:

Adventurous:

Creative:

Kind:

Difficult:

Fun:

Stupid:

Worthy:

Ingenious:

Scary:

Awesome:

Sneaky:

Tricky:

Brave:

What Bugs Me the Most!

**Bugs bug me... Bug bites bug me...
Here's what else bugs me...**

WEEK #1

Doodle Page

WEEK #2

Doodle Page

WEEK #3

Doodle Page

WeeK #4

Doodle Page

WEEK #5

Doodle Page

WEEK #6

Doodle Page

WEEK #7

Doodle Page

WEEK #8

Doodle Page

Autographs

We had good times! And we had laughs!
So now let's trade our autographs!

Remember the north. Remember the south. Remember me and my big mouth!

100

GOOD VIBES ONLY

I saw you in the ocean,
I saw you in the sea.
I saw you in the shower.
Oops! Pardon me!

Autographs

the ice screams . . . the fire escapes . . . the autumn leaves . . . the ocean waves

YOURS UNTIL

I love you, I love you, I love you, I do.

But don't get excited—I love monkeys, too!

You Must Remember This!

Biggest Laugh:

_____

_____

_____

Worst Scare:

_____

_____

_____

Best Prank:

_____

_____

_____

Best Meal:

_____

_____

_____

Most Embarrassing Moment:

Proudest Day:

Biggest Secret:

Funniest Story:

Believe It or Not!:

Names & Contact Info

Name:

Contact Info:

Name:

Contact Info:

Name:

Contact Info:

Name:

Contact Info:

Name:

Contact Info:

Name:

Contact Info:

Name:

Contact Info:

Name:

Contact Info:

Name:

Contact Info:

Name:

Contact Info:

Name:

Contact Info:

Name:

Contact Info:

Name:

Contact Info:

Name:

Contact Info:

Name:

Contact Info:

Name:

Contact Info:

Name:

Contact Info:

Name:

Contact Info:

Name:

Contact Info:

Name:

Contact Info:

Name:

Contact Info:

Name:

Contact Info:

Name:

Contact Info:

Name:

Contact Info:

Name:

Contact Info:

Name:

Contact Info:

Name:

Contact Info:

Name:

Contact Info:

Name:

Contact Info:

Name:

Contact Info:

Name:

Contact Info:

Name:

Contact Info:

Name:

Contact Info:

Name:

Contact Info: